POCKET BOOK OF
ONE-LINERS

AWESOME
INSULTS

ALLSORTED.

An exclusive edition for

for all your gift books and gift stationery

This 10th edition published in Great Britain in 2021
by Allsorted Ltd, Watford, Herts, UK WD19 4BG

Author: Roffy
Cover design: Milestone Creative
Contents layout: seagulls.net

ISBN: 978-1-910562-91-8

Printed in China

CONTENTS

INTRODUCTION 5

GETTING PERSONAL 6

PEOPLE PROBLEMS 20

BEATEN WITH THE
UGLY STICK 34

MIXED NUTTERS 46

WORKPLACE WEIRDOS 62

IF ALL ELSE FAILS 80

INTRODUCTION

Every person you meet treats you with respect.
They are honest, always complimentary and
do their utmost to make your day that little
bit brighter.

Then you wake up and have to deal with
people in the real world. Annoying, ignorant,
rude. And that's just your mum.

Whoah! What happened there??

Sorry about that – we know that your entire
family are actually wonderful people – it was
just a little demonstration of how disrespect can
creep up on you unannounced.

Thankfully you are now holding over 500 finely
honed put-downs to score a few points against
the genuinely annoying, ignorant and rude people
in your life.

But before you unleash insults on all around you,
please ask yourself if you are the smartest, most
beautiful person on earth. Oh, you are? Everyone
else is inferior? Please proceed...

GETTING PERSONAL

YOU'RE A DECENT HUMAN BEING.
YOU KNOW THAT IT'S NOT RIGHT TO
PICK ON SOMEONE JUST BECAUSE THERE
IS ONE ASPECT OF THEM THAT IS
DIFFERENT TO YOU.

They may be taller, shorter, younger or older. But no one can choose their stature (or lack of it) or age (or excess of it) so neither deserve mocking in their own right.

However, if they decide to frustrate, annoy or insult you, then they have changed the rules. The gloves are off, they've made everything fair game and it's only natural to aim for the weakest point.

And as you are the dictionary definition of 'normal', they'll have nothing to say back to you. Will they?

TALL TALES

SPEAK SLOWLY, THE AIR IS MUCH THINNER UP THERE.

- Do you eat regular food, or just nibble from the treetops?

- Can you move that cloud for me, please?

- Why don't you go and hold up some telephone wires?

- Can you drive a car that doesn't have a sunroof?

- Duck, there's an aeroplane coming.

- CAN YOU HEAR ME UP THERE??

- So what is the opposite of a dwarf then?

- Did you fall asleep in some compost?

- Can you give me a hand? I need to fix my roof and I can't afford the scaffolding.

- So who won? You or Godzilla?

SHORT STORIES

THEY ALREADY HAVE A NAPOLEON COMPLEX ANYWAY.

- If you pulled your socks up you'd be blind.

- Do your feet appear in your passport photo?

- When you were a child did your parents have to buy two booster seats?

- And which dwarf are you?

- Can you tell the difference between a headache and a foot ache?

- You could bungee jump off a kerb.

- I'll let you know when it starts to rain.

- You could pose for trophies.

- If you were any shorter, you could date Barbie.

- Everyone looks up to somebody, but you look up to everyone.

- I wouldn't make fun of your height. I couldn't stoop so low.

||||||||||||||||||||||||||||||||||||||||||||||||||||||||||||||||||||||||||||||||||||||||||||||||||||||||

WHAT'S BETWEEN THOSE FUNNY EARS?

KICK THEM STRAIGHT IN THE GREY MATTER.

- It's kinda sad watching you attempt to fit your entire vocabulary into a sentence.

- If I typed 'idiot' into Google, would I get pictures of you or your mum?

- You're not pretty enough to be this stupid.

- Scientists say the universe is made up of neutrons, protons and electrons. They forgot to mention morons.

- The gates are down, the lights are flashing and the bells are ringing – but the train isn't coming.

- Ordinarily people live and learn. You just live.

- I don't know what makes you so stupid, but it really works.

- People say that you're the perfect idiot. I say that you're not perfect but you're doing all right.

- I'm sure you fell out of the stupid tree and hit every branch on the way down.

- Sorry, but there's no vaccine against stupidity.

- A half-wit gave you a piece of his mind, and you held onto it.

- If you were any more stupid, you'd have to be watered twice a week.

- You're not stupid. You just have bad luck when thinking.

HEAVYWEIGHTS

BECAUSE THE WORLD'S POPULATION ISN'T GETTING ANY LIGHTER.

- You're so fat, you could sell shade.

- You're so fat, even your car has stretch marks.

- You're so fat, if you got your shoes shined, you'd have to take their word for it.

- You're so fat, you sweat butter.

- You're so fat, when you take a shower your feet don't get wet.

- You're so fat, even your shadow casts a shadow.

- OK, you're big boned. But your big bones are fat.

WHAT A WAIST

THEY'RE NOT FAT, THEY'RE JUST EASIER TO SEE.

- You'd do anything to lose weight. Apart from exercise or diet.

- Your eating habits are fine – if you're pregnant.

- Your portion size looks about right. For a family of four.

- You must be on the seafood diet. When you see food, you eat it.

- You have something on your chin. No, the third one down.

- You're in shape. Round is a shape.

- You may think you're fat, but you're right.

- You're the reason they invented double doors.

- At least when I do a handstand my stomach doesn't hit me in the face.

- You're a light eater, all right. As soon as it gets light, you start eating.

- It looks like you were poured into your clothes and someone forgot to say 'when'.

LIGHTWEIGHTS

THE OTHER END OF THE SCALES.

- I've seen better legs on chickens.

- You make size zero models jealous.

- Do you use dental floss for toilet paper?

- If you swallowed a meatball you'd look pregnant.

- Do your trousers have just the one belt loop?

- Don't wear a yellow top and a red beret – you'll be mistaken for a pencil.

- Can I play a tune on your rib cage?

- I guess you have to be careful not to fall through cattle grids.

- It must be fun hula-hooping with a Cheerio.

- You have threads hanging from your shorts. Oh, sorry, it's your legs.

- I wish I could dodge raindrops like you.

FASHION POLICE

WHEN THE STATEMENT THEY ARE MAKING IS 'I SHOULD BE WEARING SOMETHING ELSE'.

- Are you going to a Bad Taste Party this evening?

- Interesting shirt. Did you win the bet?

- Some people could make that top work.

- Does that shirt come with a dimmer switch?

- I'm sure it looked great in the shop.

- Did you get dressed in the dark this morning?

- Whatever kind of look you were going for, you missed.

- That tie is so ugly, it would be insulting to strangle someone with it.

- It's brave of you to wear it one more time before using it as a rag.

- Give it another five years and it might be back in fashion.

- Did you forget to change your shoes at the bowling alley?

- Your clothes attract attention. Not to mention flies.

- I had a shirt like that after the dog threw up on it.

NICE TAN. ORANGE IS MY FAVOURITE COLOUR.

I DON'T KNOW IF YOU KNOW THIS BUT YOUR BOOBS GO INSIDE YOUR CLOTHES.

THE CAMEL CALLED, HE WANTS HIS TOE BACK.

KEEP IT IN THE FAMILY

IT'S NOT JUST THEIR LOOKS, IT'S THEIR WHOLE GENETIC MAKEUP.

- You are your mum's least favourite child.

- You're the reason the gene pool needs a lifeguard.

- Your family tree must be a cactus because everybody on it is a prick.

- If you really want to know about mistakes, you should ask your parents.

- You'll never be the man your mother is.

- How's the wife and my kids?

- Sometimes you open your mouth and your mother comes out.

- Ever since I saw you in your family tree I've wanted to cut it down.

- All that you are you owe to your parents. Why don't you send them a penny and square the account?

- Did your parents ever ask you to run away from home?

- I certainly hope you are sterile.

- I guess it's not your turn with the family brain-cell.

- Your family tree is solid, but you are the sap.

- Your parents hated you so much your bath toys were an iron and a toaster.

THE YOUNG ONES

FACE IT, YOU'RE JUST JEALOUS OF THEIR YOUTH.

- Do you need your nappy changing?

- Just wait until puberty kicks in.

- So which is your favourite Power Ranger?

- I don't think you were born yesterday. At least a week last Thursday, perhaps.

- Soon you'll have hair on your chest. It'll match what's on your palms.

- When your acne clears up, you'll still look like a second-hand dartboard.

- Aww, have you run out of Haribos?

NO SPRING CHICKEN

21 AGAIN. AND AGAIN. AND AGAIN.

- Has your blood type been discontinued?

- I would ask you how old you are but I know you can't count that high.

- Does the hairdresser charge you a search fee?

- Your teeth are like stars – they come out at night.

- What was it like working on the pyramids?

- I saw the vultures circling your house.

- I'm ready to light your cake. Hand me the blowtorch.

- You don't need a plastic surgeon. You need an archaeologist.

- One more wrinkle and you'd pass for a prune.

- When you were a kid, rainbows were black and white.

- Has your birth certificate expired?

- At least with those wrinkles you can screw your hat on tight.

SOLE MAN

WHO WOULD BE A CHIROPODIST?

- Your feet smell so bad your shoes are gagging.

- Want to fight air pollution? Keep your shoes on.

- You have feet only a clown could love.

- With feet that big do you get disqualified from swimming competitions for wearing flippers?

- Did all your little piggies eat roast beef?

- Your feet stink so much your shoes hid in the cupboard and refused to come out.

- I hear your feet smell so bad that even the flies in your house wear gas masks.

- Do you need to bother with water skis?

- My lawnmower is broken. Can you walk in my garden barefoot for 20 minutes?

- Do your shoes regret having tongues?

PEOPLE PROBLEMS

DO PEOPLE CHOOSE TO BE INSULTED?
THEY MAY NOT REALISE IT, BUT IT
OFTEN SEEMS TO BE THE CASE.

Some choose to tell a bad joke. Others choose to sing in public with no discernible talent. And for some reason, there are people out there who choose the hipster lifestyle.

These choices, and others like them, are clearly open invitations for you to insult such people. In fact, they are demanding that you insult them. Let's face it, who could possibly think that bad jokes, bad singing or bad beards invite compliments? If they do think that, they have a questionable intelligence that you need to insult anyway.

It looks like you're going to be busy.

SLOTH ENVY

DON'T GET ME STARTED ABOUT GETTING STARTED.

- You're so lazy you've got a remote control just to operate your remote.

- You'd stick your nose out the window and let the wind blow it.

- You work from home and still can't get to work on time.

- You'd arrive late at your own funeral.

- Was your first question today 'Should I sit down and do nothing or should I lie down and do nothing'?

- If you were a kangaroo, you'd be a pouch potato.

- Is the only entry on your to-do list 'nothing'?

- At least you'd come first in a Netflix marathon.

- You won't even empty your computer's recycle bin.

VOICE OF AN ANGLE

WHEN THEY ARE OFF THE SCALE.

- Have you ever considered becoming a mime?

- I preferred the instrumental version.

- You should try singing in a vacuum.

- So that's how a Jackson Pollock painting sounds.

- My dog didn't howl that badly when we had him neutered.

- What did you do with the money your mother gave you for voice lessons?

- Did somebody put a cat in a blender?

- Less X-Factor, more Why-Factor.

- Flatter than a lazy hedgehog.

THAT QUESTION

NO GOOD EVER CAME OF ASKING 'DOES THIS MAKE ME LOOK FAT?'.

- It's not the dress that makes you look fat, it's the fat that makes you look fat.

- Compared to what animal?

- No it's too tight.

- There is a fine line between a dress and a sausage casing.

- Curves and rolls are not the same thing.

- It makes your muffin top look like a mushroom cloud.

- Hell no, you sexy beast, you.

- How can I answer without you punching me?

- Do I look stupid?

- You're not fat, come on, chin up. And the other one, and the other one...

HAIL TO THE CHEF

SOME PEOPLE SHOULDN'T EVEN BE ALLOWED NEAR A KETTLE.

- There's so much oil on this plate, the US is trying to invade it.

- I'm not sure which of my five senses has been offended the most.

- I never knew chocolate mousse had bones.

- How did you make this? With your hands or with your asshole?

- This crab is still singing 'Under the Sea'.

- I didn't cook in your toilet, so why did you crap on my plate?

- Interesting choice, mixing raw haggis with durian.

- This chicken is shivering and asking to have her feathers back.

- Please repeat after me – 'Sorry cow'.

- I can tie a coffee bean to my arse and swim across the Columbia River and make a darker stain than that.

- That's not a cup of tea. You've just annoyed some hot water.

BRING SEXY BACK

BECAUSE THEY TOOK IT AWAY.

- Save your breath for your inflatable girlfriend.

- My silence doesn't mean your sexual performance left me speechless.

- You're better at sex than anyone – now all you need is a partner.

- I'd rather pass a kidney stone than another night with you.

- If sex were fast food, you'd have a yellow arch over your head.

- The only way you'll ever get laid is if you crawl up a chicken's ass and wait.

- You're a real Don Juan with the ladies. The ladies Don Juan to have anything to do with you.

- You're so ugly, the only dates you get are on a calendar.

- The only thing you can turn on is the microwave.

- My straighteners are hotter than you.

- The only thing that gets turned on when you're naked is the shower.

- There's someone out there for everyone. Else.

- You owe me a drink – you're so ugly I dropped mine when I saw you.

- They say opposites attract. I hope you meet someone who is good-looking, intelligent and cultured.

JOKER'S WILD

WHEN YOU'RE LAUGHING AT THEM, NOT WITH THEM.

- Did you hurt yourself when you thought that one up?

- Should I laugh now?

- My turn. Let me give you a riddle. I wasn't listening the first time, tell me why?

- Bless. That's OK, you can try again later.

- Wow, I'd better write that one down.

- Oh, I'm sorry, was that a joke?

- I'm assuming you thought of that yourself.

- Noah called, he wants his two jokes back.

- You're not funny, but your life, now that's a joke.

EVERYDAY IDIOTS

YOU DON'T LIKE THEM, YOU CAN'T FIGURE OUT WHY. MAYBE BECAUSE THEY ARE JUST AN IDIOT.

- It sounds like English, but I can't understand a damn word you're saying.

- Did you get lost in thought? Was it unfamiliar territory?

- You must have a Teflon brain, because nothing sticks.

- I'd like to leave you with one thought, but I'm not sure you have a place to put it.

- Calling you stupid would be an insult to stupid people.

- I'm listening. It just takes me a while to process that much stupidity at once.

- When I look into your eyes, I see the back of your head.

- I'm sorry if I hurt your feelings when I called you stupid. I thought you already knew.

- I'd slap you senseless, but I can't spare three seconds.

- You're depriving some poor village of its idiot.

- He's street smart. Sesame Street smart.

- How many years did it take you to learn how to breathe?

- Bless. It's so cute when you try to talk about things you don't understand.

BOOZE LOSER

WHEN THE BARREL IS ALWAYS EMPTY.

- I didn't know you were a drunk until you turned up for work sober.

- If there was a nip in the air you'd try to drink it.

- I see you like a balanced diet – a beer in each hand.

- When you donate blood, there's so much alcohol in it, they use it to sterilise the needles.

- On your last birthday, with just one breath you lit all the candles on your birthday cake.

- It only takes one drink to make you drunk. But I'm not sure whether it's the ninth or the tenth.

- The only exercise you ever get is hiccupping.

BORRRRRING

EXCITEMENT IS NOT THEIR MIDDLE NAME.

- My hope for you is that you someday find the end of your sentence.

- You are so boring that you can't even entertain a doubt.

- Your lips keep moving but all I hear is 'Blah, blah, blah'.

- You are as interesting as a documentary on dirt.

- Talk to me. I could use the sleep.

- Sure I'm listening. Can't you see me yawning?

- I heard you talked to your plants and they died of boredom.

- It must give you a great sense of power knowing you could bore the world to death.

- I hate to leave, but my doctor says boredom is bad for me.

HIPSTER HORRORS

WE WERE INSULTING HIPSTERS BEFORE IT WAS COOL.

- Nice of your grandmother to lend you her sweater.

- Are those glasses prescription?

- I'd like to bury you in a shallow grave, but I doubt that's underground enough for you.

- Do many birds live in that beard?

- I'd like to drown you in the mainstream.

- Did your degree in media studies help you get a job as a lumberjack?

- There's a new insult about hipsters, but you've probably not heard of it.

- No matter how cool you think that new bar is, you're still an alcoholic.

- If I fart near you and your friends, will you argue over who heard it first?

ROAD RAGE

WHEN DID SIGNALLING BECOME OPTIONAL?

- You couldn't even pass a kidney stone.

- The way you pulled in makes me wish your dad pulled out.

- Oi, Pacman, pick one side of the dotted line.

- Can I assume you parked blindfolded while a badger clawed at your crotch?

- The next time you park like that you should leave a can opener so the people next to you can get out.

- When was the last time you had your eyes tested? No reason...

- Does your GPS cry?

- It takes 10,000 bolts to build a car but only one nut to drive it like that.

- I've seen a three-year-old with a colouring book stay in the lines better than you.

GAME BOYS

BECAUSE ONLINE GAMING IS FULL OF SEVEN-YEAR-OLDS WHO HAVE JUST LEARNT TO SWEAR.

- The safest place for us to stand is in front of your gun.

- Are you a decoy?

- 'Options > How To Play'

- Is your keyboard broken?

- I think you'd prefer Tetris.

- As a serious gamer, I would describe you as casual.

- Is your broadband as slow as your reactions?

- Shame you can't buy skill.

- You have one option left – uninstall.

- You should have a rest and let your mum take over.

BEATEN WITH THE UGLY STICK

STUDIES SHOW THAT 78% OF PEOPLE ARE ANXIOUS ABOUT THEIR LOOKS.* IT'S EASY TO SEE WHY.

Advertisements scorn us for not plastering ourselves in a bucket of pseudoscientific products to conquer every tiny flaw. And you need different ones throughout the day – morning moisturiser, lunchtime moisturiser, afternoon moisturiser, five minutes to eight moisturiser – the list is endless.

But such anxiety means that it is quite easy to insult someone's appearance. That's why this chapter comes with a warning. It is the truly bitchy section of the book.

We recommend you study it in detail, memorise every single insult within and use each whenever possible. And, if you are willing to put in the effort, you too can become a walking celebrity gossip magazine.

* Other studies show that 84% of people will readily accept any printed statistics as fact, even made up ones.

FACE TIME

WHEN IT LOOKS LIKE THEIR FEATURES WERE ARRANGED BY PICASSO. WHILE HE WAS ASLEEP.

- There's only one problem with your face – I can see it.

- Your face makes onions cry.

- If my dog had your face, I would shave his butt and make him walk backwards.

- You have a very sympathetic face. It has everyone's sympathy.

- If you put your face by the door, no one would ever come in.

- Your face is very becoming... Becoming more and more ugly every time I see it.

- If I had a face like yours, I'd sue my parents.

- If laughter is the best medicine, your face might cure the world.

- Do bank robbers stop and give you their masks to wear?

- You have a striking face. Tell me, how many times were you struck there?

- You have the perfect face for radio.

- Know what goes well with your face?
  A paper bag.

- I am not going to say mean things about your looks. Your face speaks for itself.

U. G. L. Y.

WHEN THERE'S NO OTHER WORD FOR IT.

- Don't you need a licence to be that ugly?

- Did something bad happen to you or are you just naturally ugly?

- I don't want you to turn the other cheek. It's just as ugly.

- You should have been born in the Dark Ages; you look terrible in the light.

- Women like your body. They like it to go away.

- Can I have your picture? I want to scare my sister.

- Did you get fired from the Ghost Train for being too scary?

- Mirrors can't talk, and lucky for you they can't laugh either.

GETTING SPECIFIC

IT'S LIKELY THEY KNOW WHAT'S COMING.

- You have such a big mouth you could sing a duet all by yourself.

- Your teeth are like the Ten Commandments – all broken.

- You have a Roman nose. It seems to roam all over your face.

- Keep away from major sporting events. With those ears they might confuse your head for the trophy.

- Your smile really brightens up my day, perhaps because your teeth are so yellow.

- Is that your nose or did kids throw tomatoes at you again?

- Don't look up. Your nose might poke a hole in the ozone layer.

- Can you pick up a peanut with that nose?

- You have a nice head on your shoulders. But it would look better on a neck.

- The only thing grosser than your nose is what's inside it.

DO YOUR EARS
PICK UP ALIEN
SIGNALS?

I'VE SEEN
NICER HEADS
ON A WITCH
DOCTOR'S BELT.

A BALD SPOT IS
NOTHING TO BE
EMBARRASSED
ABOUT. IT'S
JUST WHERE
YOUR SOUL LEFT
YOUR BODY.

STRAIGHT TO THE POINT

BEFORE YOU UNLEASH, CHECK YOU ARE AN OIL PAINTING YOURSELF.

- You're so ugly Hello Kitty said goodbye to you.

- You're so ugly that when you were born the doctor threw you out the window and the window threw you back.

- You're so ugly that when you went to a haunted house they offered you a job.

- You're so ugly you almost look like your mother.

- You're so ugly you have to trick or treat over the phone.

- You're so ugly you make blind kids cry.

- You're so ugly you had tinted windows on your incubator.

- You're so ugly that when you look in the mirror, your reflection looks away.

- You're so ugly that at a Christmas party they hung you up and kissed the mistletoe.

- You're so ugly you have to dress up as a brick to get laid.

ABOUT FACE

BECAUSE THEY REMIND YOU OF SOMETHING. AND AN UGLY SOMETHING AT THAT.

- You look like a 'before' picture.

- You have a face like a flower. A cauliflower.

- What's it like being a gargoyle model?

- The last time I saw a face like yours I fed it a banana.

- Wow, your face reminds me of a famous movie star – Shrek.

- It looks like your face caught fire, and someone tried to put it out with a fork.

- Can I borrow your face for a few days while my arse is on holiday?

- I hear you're very kind to animals, so please give that face back to the gorilla.

- Is that your face? Or did your neck just throw up?

- Your face rings a bell. Or do you remind me of Quasimodo?

- You look good. For roadkill.

I GUESS YOU FEEL DEAD ON THE INSIDE, WHICH MAKES SENSE BECAUSE THAT'S HOW YOU LOOK ON THE OUTSIDE TOO.

PERSONALITY CRISIS

WHEN THEY ARE UGLY ON THE INSIDE.

- You would think with all of your multiple personalities, at least one would be likeable.

- You should do some soul-searching. Maybe you'll find one.

- You shouldn't play hide and seek, no one would look for you.

- You're shallower than a dry seabed.

- If your personality were any less colourful, you'd be invisible.

- Your face looks fine, but you'll have to put a bag over that personality.

- It's not that people don't like you, it's just that you're unlikeable.

- Did the aliens forget to remove your anal probe?

- No need to charge your phone, nobody's going to call.

- Even misery doesn't love your company.

- You're a legend in your own mirror.

HAIRDOS AND HAIRDON'TS

SOME PEOPLE WOULD JUST LOOK BETTER BALD.

- The 80s called. They want their haircut back.

- It's such a shame to ruin your beautiful blonde hair by dying your roots black.

- Nice hair. Still styling it with a strimmer?

- I've seen better hair clogging my shower drain.

- Did your cat cough up your new hairstyle?

- Why don't you do something different with your hair? Like wash it.

- I'm sure the sparrows love living in there.

- I suddenly crave a bowl of shredded wheat.

- Did you confuse your shampoo with WD-40 again?

- Nice hairdo. But isn't it early for Halloween?

- He has wavy hair – it's waving goodbye.

- Didn't have time to do your hair this morning then?

SKIN DEEP

LOOKS AREN'T EVERYTHING. IN THEIR CASE, THEY AREN'T ANYTHING.

- Not so much a siren, as a false alarm.

- Your hockey team made you goalie so you'd have to wear a mask.

- I was going to give you a nasty look, but you already have one.

- If I got a penny for everyone I've met who is as beautiful as you, I'd have all the money in the world.

- I'm not as dumb as you look.

- I don't know where you got your looks, but I hope you kept the receipt.

- So you're the reason photoshop was invented.

- If beauty is skin deep, you're inside out.

- I'd insult you, but I won't do as well as nature did.

- You have that faraway look. The further you get, the better you look.

MIXED NUTTERS

THE SAYING GOES 'HE DOESN'T
SUFFER FOOLS GLADLY'. BUT THIS BEGS
THE QUESTION, WHO DOES? WHAT KIND
OF PERSON WOULD WELCOME IDIOTS
WITH OPEN ARMS? THE FACT THAT YOU
TURNED TO THIS SECTION SUGGESTS IT'S
NOT YOU. IT ACTUALLY SUGGESTS
QUITE THE OPPOSITE.

Would it be fair to say that your days are littered with numbskulls who insist on making your life just that little bit more challenging?

Yes. We thought so. That's why there is a whole chapter of one-liners to throw the way of the synaptically challenged.

Unfortunately, they may too stupid to realise they are being insulted. In that case, be prepared to suffer the fools, gladly or not.

NOT THE FULL LOAD

BECAUSE THEY ARE CLEARLY MISSING SOMETHING.

- A few nuts short of a full pouch.
- A few clowns short of a circus.
- A few fries short of a Happy Meal.
- A beer short of a six-pack.
- A few carrots short of a casserole.
- A few feathers short of a whole duck.
- A few bricks short of a hod.
- A few stars short of a constellation.
- A cornflake short of a breakfast.
- A topping short of a pizza.
- A fruitcake short of Christmas.
- A lightbulb short of a chandelier.
- A neuron short of a synapse.
- An olive short of a martini.

BRAIN DRAIN

WHEN THE WHOLE THING IS MISSING IN ACTION.

- If you had another brain, it would be lonely.

- At least you don't have to worry about a zombie apocalypse.

- Brains aren't everything. In your case, they're nothing.

- How much refund do you expect on your head now that it's empty?

- If brains were rain, you'd be a desert.

- Did you donate your brain to science before you'd finished using it?

- You have two brains, but one is lost and the other is out looking for it.

- There's a twinkle in your eyes. It's actually the sun shining between your ears.

- If I stand close enough to you, I can hear the ocean.

GREY MATTERS

WHEN THE SIZE OR QUALITY IS TO BLAME.

- Don't let your mind wander. It's too little to be let out alone.

- Careful now, don't let your brains go to your head!

- So, a thought crossed your mind? Must have been a long and lonely journey.

- I see today you have something on your mind – you're wearing a hat.

- If brains were dynamite you wouldn't have enough to blow your nose.

- I look into your eyes and get the feeling someone else is driving.

- I'd like to pick your brain, but I don't have tweezers that small.

- Can I borrow your brain? You're obviously not using it.

- At least you'll never have a mental breakdown – there are no moving parts up there.

NOT
THAT

WHEN YOU NEED TO RULE OUT SOME OPTIONS.

- Not the sharpest knife in the drawer.
- Not the brightest light in the harbour.
- Not the quickest bunny in the forest.
- Not the brightest bulb on the Christmas tree.
- Not the sharpest cheese in the bin.
- Not the brightest crayon in the box.
- Not the sharpest tool in the shed.
- Not the quickest horse in the stable.
- Not the fastest car on the track.
- Not the crunchiest crisp in the bag.
- Not the brightest button on the blouse.

WHAT'S WRONG WITH THEM?

THERE MUST BE A REASON FOR THIS.

- His chimney's clogged.

- She doesn't have all her dogs on one leash.

- His elevator doesn't go all the way to the top floor.

- She forgot to pay her brain bill.

- His aerial is pointing the wrong way.

- Her sewing machine's out of thread.

- His belt doesn't go through all the loops.

- She's missing a few buttons on her remote control.

- There's no grain in his silo.

- Her call is still on hold.

- He has less going on upstairs than a one-storey house.

- Her skylight leaks a little.

- His slinky's kinked.

- Her muesli is all nuts.

- The cheese slid off his cracker.

- There's a tiny tear in her marble bag.

- His brain waves fall a little short of the beach.

- Her suitcase doesn't have a handle.

DEMONSTRABLY DUMB

WHEN YOU NEED PROOF BY EXAMPLE.

- You're so stupid you eat soup with a fork.

- You're so stupid you would argue with a signpost.

- You're so stupid you don't know whether to scratch your watch or wind your behind.

- You're so stupid you couldn't find your way out of a paper bag.

- You're so stupid your lips move when you watch TV.

- You're so stupid you got hit by a parked car.

- You're so stupid your dog teaches you tricks.

- You're so stupid you couldn't hit water if you fell out of a boat.

- You're so stupid you'd lose a debate with a doorknob.

I WOULD LOVE TO INSULT YOU, BUT THAT WOULD BE BEYOND THE LEVEL OF YOUR INTELLIGENCE.

CHECK THE LEVELS

DO THEY EVEN KNOW WHAT AN I.Q. IS?

- Are you an experiment in Artificial Stupidity?

- Did your I.Q. test come back negative?

- Your I.Q. is room temperature.

- If ignorance is bliss, you must be the happiest person on earth.

- Some drink from the fountain of knowledge. You only gargled.

- You have the I.Q. of cheese.

- Converse with any plankton lately?

- You are a person of rare intelligence. Well, it's rare when you show any.

- You are one I.Q. point above brain death.

- They can't measure your intelligence. The scale won't go that low.

- I don't have the time or the crayons to explain it to you.

- When your I.Q. reaches 50, you should sell.

- You're the reason we have to put instructions on toothpaste.

THAT EXPLAINS IT

ARE THEY TOO STUPID TO SPOT SUBTLETY?

- The driveway doesn't quite reach the road.
- The battery isn't fully charged.
- He doesn't have all the chairs at the table.
- She's knitting with only one needle.
- A few roos loose in the top paddock.
- The wind is blowing but nothing is moving.
- The boat doesn't have all the oars in the water.
- Hasn't seen the ball since kickoff.
- Shipped but not delivered.
- Nice house, not much furniture.
- Batteries not included.
- Lost contact with the mothership.
- The corn bread isn't done in the middle.
- The lights are on but no one's home.
- Not wrapped too tight.
- Not all the dots are on the dice.
- Nice cage, but no bird.
- That bats are out of the belfry.

THE DIPSTICK DOESN'T REACH THE OIL.

THE PILOT LIGHT HAS GONE OUT.

THERE'S NO NET BETWEEN THE GOAL POSTS.

I KNOW I'M TALKING LIKE AN IDIOT.
I HAVE TO, OTHERWISE YOU WOULDN'T UNDERSTAND WHAT I'M SAYING.

TOO BAD STUPIDITY ISN'T PAINFUL.

STUPID IS AS STUPID DOES

IT'S LIKE THEY ARE TRYING TO BE THAT DUMB.

- Are you always so stupid or is today a special occasion?

- I would engage in a battle of wits with you, but I never attack someone who is unarmed.

- Keep on trying – one day you might make it to moron.

- You look tired. Have you been thinking?

- If I wanted to hurt myself, I'd climb up to your ego and jump down to your I.Q. level.

- I've had more meaningful conversations with a brick wall.

- You're a gross ignoramus – 144 times worse than an ordinary ignoramus.

- Everyone's entitled to be stupid, but you're abusing the privilege

- I know you are nobody's fool but maybe someone will adopt you.

- If I gave you a penny for your thoughts, you'd owe me change.

STILL COMING UP SHORT

WHAT ELSE IS MISSING?

- A few screws short of a hardware store.
- A few cards short of a deck.
- A few keys short of a keyboard.
- A few threads short of a sweater.
- A few sandwiches short of a picnic.
- A few Bradys short of a Bunch.
- A few burgers short of a barbecue.
- A few shades short of a rainbow.
- A few bristles short of a broom.
- A few players short of a team.
- A few sheep short of a flock.
- A few gunmen short of a posse.
- A few bits short of a byte.
- A few cowboys short of a rodeo.
- A few grapes short of a fruit salad.
- A few whiskers short of a kitten.

SLOW, SLOW, QUICK QUICK, SLOW

I'M NOT COMPARING THEE TO A SUMMER'S DAY.

- About as sharp as a marble.

- Smart as a bag of rocks.

- As smart as a stick.

- Sharp as a sack of wet mice.

- Dumber than a bag of hammers.

- Dumb as a stump.

- As sharp as a pound of wet liver.

- A quick as a snail crossing superglue.

- As sharp as a mashed potato.

- Slow as a slug on dope.

- Slower than dial-up.

- As smart as bait.

WORKPLACE WEIRDOS

YOU SPEND SO MUCH OF YOUR LIFE AT WORK, IT'S NOT SURPRISING THAT THERE ARE TIMES IT GETS A LITTLE FRUSTRATING. EVEN IF IT'S YOUR PERFECT JOB, THERE ARE MOMENTS WHEN YOU FEEL YOUR BOSS, YOUR COLLEAGUES OR YOUR CUSTOMERS DESERVE THE ROUGH SIDE OF YOUR TONGUE.

But is it a good idea to unleash insults in all directions? Your boss pays your wages, you need the support of your colleagues and your customers need to be kept happy at all costs.

Of course it's a good idea. It's work, so it's not an 'insult', it's 'banter'.

Speak your mind at work. Tell them all exactly what you think of them. And if they don't appreciate it, they don't deserve you. There are plenty more places you can get a job. No one checks references anyway. Do they? Oh...

9 TO 5

WHY NOT INSULT EVERYTHING ABOUT YOUR JOB AND YOUR COLLEAGUES IN ONE GO?

- If idiots could fly, this would be an airport.

- This isn't an office. It's Hell with fluorescent lighting.

- Can I trade this job for what's in box number 1?

- A cubicle is just a padded cell without a door.

- I hate my job, but it pays for my alcohol. I need the alcohol because I hate my job.

- My people skills would be better if I was surrounded by better people.

- Do I get a promotion if I last here for a week without stabbing anyone with a fork?

- Now I understand why Batman prefers working alone.

THAT GUY

EVERY WORKPLACE HAS ONE.

- The cream rises to the top. So does the scum.

- He sets low personal standards and then consistently fails to achieve them.

- The only thing he brought to this job was his car.

- He started at the bottom – and it's been downhill ever since.

- He dines with the top brass – they don't trust him with the silver.

- He's the kind of guy you'd really like to run into sometime. With your car.

- He's a man of few words. Trouble is, he keeps repeating them.

- No one can call him a quitter – he's always been fired from every job he's had.

- His head is so far up his ass he can chew his food twice.

- Some people are has-beens. He is a never-was.

MEETINGS, MEETINGS, MEETINGS

A LITTLE LESS CONVERSATION, A LITTLE MORE ACTION PLEASE.

- You only open your mouth to change your foot.

- And your whiny, half-arsed opinion would be?

- That's a great idea. Why don't you stick it in an envelope and post it to last week when we could have used it?

- If I wanted to listen to an asshole I'd fart.

- I could eat a bowl of alphabet soup and crap out a better argument than that.

- Do you want my honest opinion or a compliment?

- You are unanimous in your own opinion.

- So you've changed your mind. Does this one work any better?

- Can we get this over with? I have some proper work to do.

- This is not so much a brainstorm as a slight drizzle.

HERE, LET ME CLEAN THE BROWN OFF YOUR NOSE.

I'M NOT CONVINCED WE'VE WASTED ENOUGH TIME ON THIS YET.

I'D LIKE TO SEE THINGS FROM YOUR POINT OF VIEW, BUT I CAN'T SEEM TO GET MY HEAD THAT FAR UP YOUR ARSE.

FAILURE IS ALL YOU'RE ACTUALLY GOOD AT, BUT YOU'RE REALLY GOOD AT IT.

DAMNED WITH FAINT PRAISE

BECAUSE NEGGING IS NOT JUST FOR RELATIONSHIPS.

- Good work, I can really tell what you were trying to do.

- Thank you. We're all refreshed and challenged by your unique point of view.

- You've done really well for someone with your abilities.

- You did better than I expected.

- You're really living up to your potential. Keep at it.

- You're filling a much-needed gap in the team.

- You're at the top of the bell curve.

- I'm pleasantly surprised you kept up.

- I really appreciate how clever you think you are.

- Well done – soon you will appear to be competent.

- I can see how someone like you would think that.

- I like the font.

UNDERWORKED, OVERPAID

THOSE MOTIVATIONAL POSTERS DON'T WORK FOR EVERYONE.

- If procrastination was an Olympic sport, you'd start the training tomorrow.

- If you were any later, you'd be on time for tomorrow.

- I didn't realise we were playing statues.

- Is your spirit guide a three-toed sloth?

- Don't burn yourself out from all the work you do.

- Working hard or hardly working?

- Just like a blister, you show up when the work is done.

- Carry on with what you're doing – YouTube isn't going to watch itself.

- I didn't realise your mouse came with a snooze button.

ALL MOUTH

WHEN THEIR LIPS JUST DON'T STOP FLAPPING.

- If only you could make your mind work as fast as your mouth.

- You have a waterproof voice. No one can drown it out.

- Why don't you shut up and give that hole in your face a chance to heal?

- I love the sound you make when you shut up.

- You're like a novelty tie – loud and useless.

- I think I heard you say 'Blah, blah, blah, blah'. Is that right?

- Are you still me-deep in conversation?

- You've got tongue enough for ten rows of teeth.

- You're the reason I need headphones.

- Your mouth is getting too big for your muzzle.

SOCIAL MEDIA MANAGER – PLAYS ON FACEBOOK ALL DAY.

CONSULTANT – SOLVES NOTHING WHILE MAKING MONEY PROLONGING THE PROBLEM.

OCCUPATIONAL HAZARDS

KICK THEM STRAIGHT IN THE JOB.

- Graphic Designer – likes drawing and colouring in.

- Architect – likes drawing, not so much the colouring in.

- Dentist – couldn't be bothered going past week one at medical school.

- Vet – a sociopath who wanted to be a doctor.

- Pilot – knows how to find the Autopilot button.

- Teacher – couldn't face the real world.

- PE Teacher – those who can do, those who can't teach. Those who can't teach, teach PE.

- Banker – (censored)

- Model – equally pompous about their looks and ignorant about their I.Q.

- Actor – a model who can fake crying.

- Dancer – someone whose brain doesn't move as quickly as their body.

- Financial Analyst – pretentious accountant.

- Historian – failed at maths.

UNDERQUALIFIED

YOU PAY PEANUTS, YOU GET MONKEYS.

- You're like one of those 'idiot savants', except without the 'savant' part.

- The fact that no one understands you doesn't mean you're an artist.

- I see the screw-up fairy has visited us again.

- You said you'd be in bright and early. Well, you're early.

- You couldn't find your bottom with both hands.

- I am only responsible for what I said, not for what you understand.

- You couldn't pour water out of a boot with the instructions printed on the heel.

- You'd be out of your depth in a puddle.

- It's hard to get the big picture when you have such a small screen.

- Make a mental note... oh, I see you're out of paper.

ORGANISATIONAL SKILLS

WHAT CAN THEY ORGANISE?

- You couldn't organise a piss-up in a brewery.

- You couldn't organise a fart in a curry-eating contest.

- You couldn't organise a tea party in a doll's house.

- You couldn't organise a spark in a tinderbox.

- You couldn't organise a bonfire in a lumberyard.

- You couldn't organise a shower in a rainstorm.

- You couldn't organise a two-car parade.

- You couldn't organise a fire in a match factory.

- You couldn't organise an easily organisable event even if supplied with all the resources and funding you need.

WHEN I LOOK AT YOU, I CAN'T THINK OF THE WORST PART OF GETTING OLDER – BECAUSE EVERYTHING ABOUT IT SEEMS EQUALLY BAD.

BIRTHDAY BLUES

SIGN THIS BIRTHDAY CARD PLEASE. WHO IS IT FOR? I DON'T KNOW, JUST SIGN IT.

- Another year older, but keep smiling! While you still have teeth.

- Only 35? Oh, OK.

- I have no idea who you are. Happy Birthday. Where's the cake?

- OLD means Obsolete, Lazy and Dull. Congratulations for turning one year OLDer.

- Age both adds years to your life and subtracts years from your life. Either way, it's never good news.

- Don't worry, I am right here by your side to help you mourn the death of your youth.

- Receiving a birthday message from me has undoubtedly been your biggest achievement this year.

- My condolences.

- Good luck in your next job. Oh, sorry, that's for the card you're getting next week.

HOW USEFUL?

BECAUSE NOT EVERYONE IS AS MULTITALENTED AS YOU.

- You're as useful as a windscreen wiper on a camel's arse.

- You're as useful as an ashtray on a motorcycle.

- You're as useful as ejector seats on a helicopter.

- You're as useful as a knitted condom.

- You're as useful as a glass hammer.

- You're as useful as a concrete parachute.

- You're as useful as a wooden frying-pan.

- You're as useful as Anne Frank's drum kit.

- You're as useful as rubber lips on a woodpecker.

- You're as useful as a chocolate teapot.

- You're as useful as handles on a snowball.

MISMANAGEMENT

BECAUSE ONLY THE PEOPLE WHO DESERVE PROMOTIONS GET THEM. AHEM.

- Success hasn't changed you a bit – you're still the same asshole you always were.

- You're getting carried away with your own self-importance. Unfortunately, not far enough.

- Success hasn't gone to your head – just your mouth.

- Soon you'll be selling furniture for a living. Your own.

- Congratulations on being promoted to another department. I'll really miss doing all your work.

- I'd follow you anywhere, but only out of morbid curiosity.

- He's risen to the level of his own incompetence.

- I knew you'd go far. I hope you stay there.

- Someday you'll go far, if you catch the right train.

IF ALL
ELSE FAILS

SO THERE'S SOMETHING ABOUT THEM,
BUT YOU CAN'T QUITE PUT YOUR FINGER
ON IT. IT'S NOT THEIR FUNNY LOOKS,
THEIR PERSONALITY PROBLEMS, THEIR
QUESTIONABLE SKILLS OR THEIR
SUB-PAR INTELLIGENCE.

But there is that niggly something that just grates away. And away. And away.

There's nothing to worry about, it just requires a different tactic. While you can't aim a laser-sighted insult directly at their weakest point, you can instead fire insult buckshot to ensure they don't get away unharmed.

Consider this final selection your emergency munitions dump. A selection of insults to let them know they are annoying, they should go away, and to point out that the root cause of their problem lies in their ancestry.

Alternatively, you could just regress to being a five-year-old and call them a poo-poo head.

EXIT STAGE LEFT

INSULT THEM WHILE TELLING THEM TO GO AWAY – BONUS.

- Excellent time to become a missing person.

- I like your approach, now let's see your departure.

- Have a nice day. Somewhere else.

- Leave now why I can still act like I care.

- Take a hike. Preferably to the Bermuda Triangle.

- I'll miss you like I miss Poison Ivy.

- Let's not see each other for a while. Say, for the rest of our lives.

- Goodbye. I'm so sorry you could come.

- The fun's just starting, so you must be going.

- It won't be the same without you. It will be better.

- I think you'd enjoy spending time with you.

- I'd like to help you out. Which way did you come in?

- If I promise to miss you, will you go away?

- Roses are red, violets are blue, I have five fingers, the third one's for you.

- Why don't you slip into something more comfortable... like a coma.

- I'd hate to see you go, but I'd love to watch you leave.

- I'd like to give you a going-away present, but you have to do your part first.

BACK AT YOU

BE PREPARED IF SOMEONE TRIES TO INSULT YOU. THOUGH I CAN'T THINK WHY THEY WOULD...

- I'm sorry I didn't get that, I don't speak idiot.

- And you're such a beautiful, wonderful, intelligent person. Oh I'm sorry, I thought we were having a lying competition.

- I've been called worse by better.

- I've had snappier comebacks from a bowl of Rice Krispies.

- I'm sorry, was I meant to be offended? The only thing offending me is your face.

MOONLIGHT
BECOMES
YOU. TOTAL
DARKNESS
EVEN MORE.

SOMEONE
SAID YOU
WEREN'T FIT
TO SLEEP
WITH PIGS.
I STUCK UP
FOR THE PIGS.

BACKHANDERS

DRIVE STRAIGHT TOWARDS A COMPLIMENT, THEN PULL A HANDBRAKE TURN.

- You look so good that I didn't recognise you.

- I love how you don't care what you look like.

- You're smarter than you look.

- I wish I were confident enough to wear something so inappropriate.

- I can't believe your boyfriend left you.

- You look gorgeous, like a different person.

- You're lucky you're pretty.

- I like you. You remind me of myself when I was young and stupid.

- You look really good for someone who eats horribly, doesn't exercise and drinks too much.

- I don't think you are a fool. But then what's MY opinion against thousands of others?

- I like you. People say I've no taste, but I like you.

- You are as strong as an ox and almost as intelligent.

- You're not yourself today. I noticed the improvement immediately.

HOW VERY ANNOYING

DON'T GET ANGRY. JUST GET INSULTING.

- You're driving me crazy, and taking the scenic route.

- If you're here – who's running Hell?

- I never forget a face, but in your case I'll be glad to make an exception.

- Next time I see you, remind me not to talk to you.

- What am I? Flypaper for freaks?

- I'll try being nicer if you'll try being smarter.

- Before you came along we were hungry. Now we're fed up.

- I've come across decomposed bodies that are less offensive than you are.

- I've only got one nerve left, and you're getting on it.

- You remind me of the ocean – you make me sick.

- Your doctor called with your colonoscopy results. Good news – they found your head.

- You're good for people's health. When they see you coming, they take long walks.

- I wouldn't pee in your ear if your brain was on fire.

- You are a treasure. Let's bury you.

- The trouble with you is that you're alive.

PLAYGROUND

WHEN YOU CAN'T MUSTER UP AN ADULT INSULT.

- You smell of wee.

- Four-eyes.

- Doofus.

- Snot bubble.

- You're a stupid-head.

- Made you look, made you stare, made you lose your underwear.

- Brick wall, waterfall, oh you think you know it all.

- Ewwww.

- Your face.

- Your mum.

ORIGIN STORIES

THEY'VE CLEARLY HAD THEIR PROBLEMS SINCE BIRTH. OR BEFORE.

- Some babies were dropped on their heads, you were clearly thrown at a wall.

- I would have been your dad but a dog beat me to it.

- Two wrongs don't make a right. Take your parents as an example.

- You must've been conceived in the kitchen, because that's where most accidents happen.

- All of your ancestors must number in the millions; it's hard to believe that many people are to blame for producing you.

- We all spring from apes but you didn't spring far enough.

- I bet your mother has a loud bark.

- Your birth certificate is an apology letter from the condom factory.

- Do you know how long it takes for your mother to take a crap? Nine months.

- 100,000 sperm and you were the fastest?

- I think we met in a past life and you were a dipstick then too.

WELL AREN'T YOU A WASTE OF TWO BILLION YEARS OF EVOLUTION?

AS AN OUTSIDER, WHAT DO YOU THINK OF THE HUMAN RACE?

YOU'RE THE KIND OF PERSON THAT OTHERS WOULD USE AS A BLUEPRINT TO BUILD AN IDIOT.

YOU'RE PROOF THAT EVOLUTION CAN GO IN REVERSE.

DOPES, DUMMIES AND DOLTS

WHEN THEY ARE SO DENSE THAT LIGHT BENDS AROUND THEM.

- If you're going to be a smartarse then you have to be smart. Otherwise you are just an arse.

- I just stepped in something that was smarter than you. It smelled better too.

- Why is it acceptable for you to be an idiot but not for me to point it out?

- Stupidity is not a crime, so you're free to go.

- It's a condescending thing, dear. You wouldn't understand.

- At our meeting of minds, I'm not sure if yours even turned up.

- You're not the dumbest person I've ever met, but that's only because I've met your mum.

- Did you stop to think, and forget to start again?

- I didn't say you were stupid. I said you are stupid. There's nothing past tense about it.

- You have the right to remain silent because whatever you say will probably be stupid anyway.

POINT OF VIEW

BECAUSE YOUR OPINION MATTERS. TO YOU.

- I'll never forget the first time we met – although I'll keep trying.

- There are several people in this world that I find obnoxious and you are all of them.

- I'm jealous of all the people that haven't met you.

- I don't exactly hate you, but if you were on fire and I had water, I'd drink it.

- The highlight of our friendship was unfriending you.

- I could say nice things about you, but I'd rather tell the truth.

- I'd slap you, but I don't want to get slut on my hand.

- Sorry, I thought I was dealing with an adult.

- I'm trying to imagine you with a personality.

- Believe me, I don't want to make a monkey out of you. Why should I take all the credit?

- Of all the people I've met you're certainly one of them.

- I thought of you today. It reminded me to take the bins out.

- Words can't explain it. So I'll just go and throw up.
- Sorry, I can't think of an insult stupid enough for you.
- On a scale of 1 to 10, you're a zero.
- If you were my phone, I'd look for an upgrade.
- I'm not sure which of your two faces to slap first.

QUESTIONABLE

ARE THESE RHETORICAL?

- Is that perfume or marinade?
- Is the only place you're ever invited, 'outside'?
- The next time you shave, could you stand a little closer to the razor?
- Hi there, I'm a human being! What are you?
- Is it time for your medication or mine?
- How did you get here? Did someone leave your cage open?
- I hear you changed your mind! What did you do with the nappy?
- How do you manage to both suck and blow?

WHAT ARE YOU?

SHORT AND TO THE POINT.

- You spanner.
- You pilchard.
- You numpty.
- You wazzock.
- You dork.
- You nerd.
- You wally.
- You berk.
- You plonker.
- You muppet.
- You pleb.
- You dipstick.
- You pudding.
- You spud.
- You doughnut.
- You noodle.

A WELCOME BREAK

WHO INVITED THEM ANYWAY?

- As welcome as a turd in a swimming pool.

- As welcome as a hole in a lifeboat.

- As welcome as a rattlesnake at a square dance.

- As welcome as a fart in a space suit.

- As welcome as a dog in a game of skittles.

- As welcome as a skunk at a picnic.

- As welcome as a visit from the mother-in-law.

- As welcome as an apostrophe in a bag of potatoe's.

- As welcome as a boot in the backside.

- As welcome as a mariachi band on the morning after.

- As welcome as a hedgehog in a condom factory.

POTENT PUT-DOWNS

A FINAL BATCH OF INDISCRIMINATE INSULTS.

- When you die you'll be buried face down so you can see where you're going.

- Somewhere out there is a tree, tirelessly producing oxygen so you can breathe. I think you owe it an apology.

- I'll leave you alone. Darwin will take care of you.

- I don't know what your problem is, but I'll bet it's hard to pronounce.

- Any friend of yours, is a friend of yours.

- Anyone who told you to be yourself couldn't have given you worse advice.

- Everyone is gifted. Some open the package sooner.

- If crap was music, you'd be a brass band.

- Let's play horse. I'll be the front end and you be yourself.

- Perhaps your whole purpose in life is simply to serve as a warning to others.